This book belongs to

_____

This book is dedicated to my children - Mikey, Kobe, and Jojo.

Copyright © 2025 Grow Grit Press LLC. All rights reserved. No part of this book may be reproduced in any form without permission in writing from the publisher. Please send bulk order requests to info@ninjalifehacks.tv

Paperback ISBN: 979-8-89614-051-1
Hardcover ISBN: 979-8-89614-053-5
eBook ISBN: 979-8-89614-052-8

Printed and bound in the USA.
NinjaLifeHacks.tv

Ninja Life Hacks®
by Mary Nhin

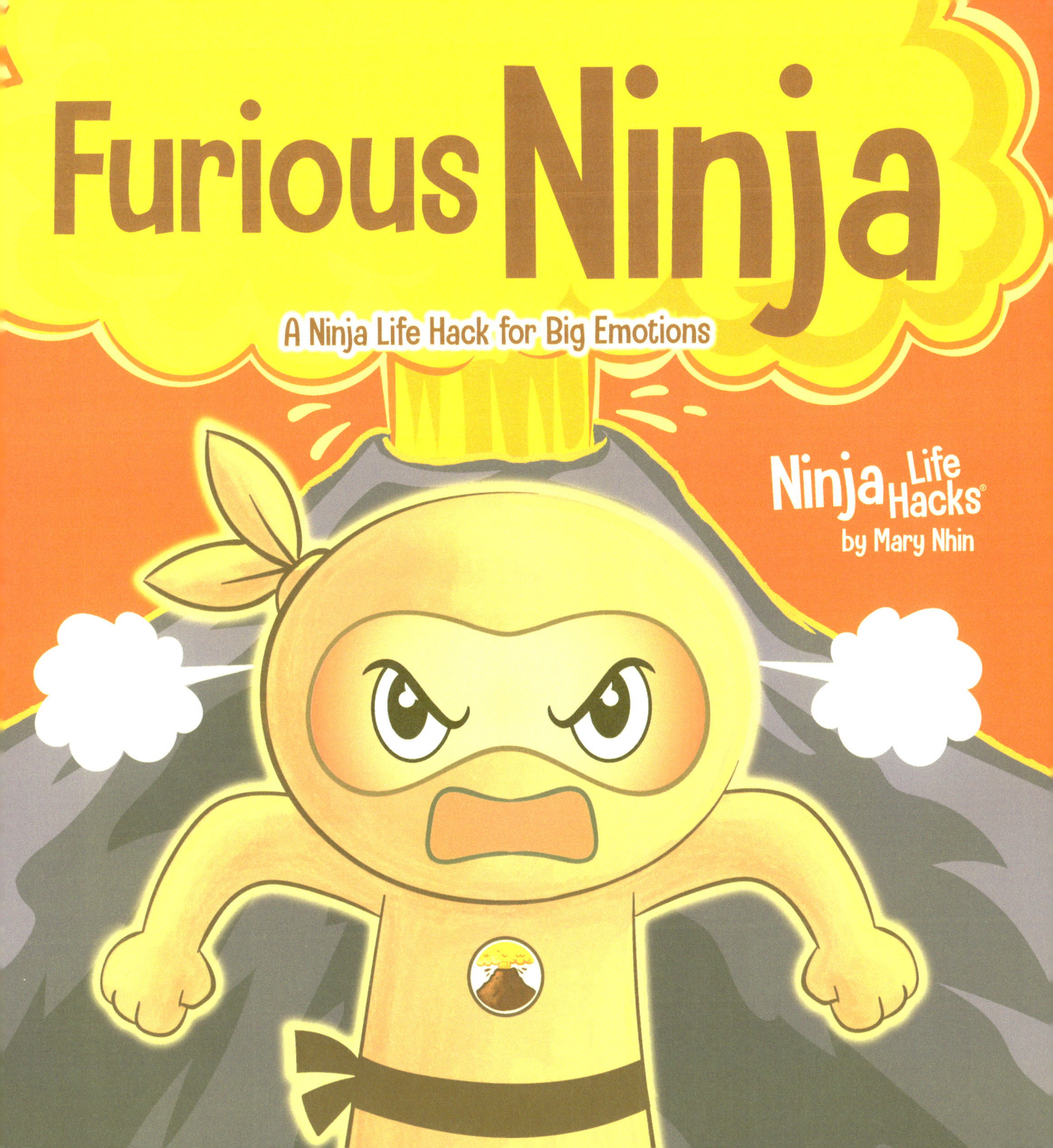

When I'm playing a game and someone cheats, I get so mad I want to scream at them. Then I remember to count to ten, and soon, I don't feel as angry anymore. I realize it's better to stay calm.

When I lose in a race, I feel like kicking the ground in frustration. I remind myself to adjust my attitude. Winning isn't everything and I had fun. That's what matters.

I didn't always know how to handle my fury. When I was younger, I would shout or stomp whenever I got mad, and it never made me feel better. In fact, it often made things worse.

Another time, I got furious at my friend for not sharing. I yelled at her, and she walked away. I felt lonely and even angrier with myself.

Then one day, Calm Ninja shared a life hack with me on how to manage my fury using the C.A.L.M. technique.

Furious Ninja, it's okay to feel angry. But remember, how you handle it is important. Try this:

C: Count to Ten - Pause and count slowly to ten.

A: Allow Yourself to Feel all the Feelings - It's okay to be mad, but you have control over your reaction.

L: Listen to Your Body - Notice how your body feels and take deep breaths to relax.

M: Make a Positive Choice - Choose a calm response instead of letting your anger take over.

Check out the fun Furious Ninja lesson plans at ninjalifehacks.tv

I love to hear from my readers. Email me your feedback or thoughts on what my next story should be at info@ninjalifehacks.tv   Yours truly, Mary

 @marynhin   @GrowGrit
#NinjaLifeHacks

 Mary Nhin   Ninja Life Hacks

 Ninja Life Hacks

 @officialninjalifehacks